RANSOMED:
Let the redeemed of the LORD say so...
By
William Stewart Whittemore

"Let the redeemed of the LORD say so,
Whom He has redeemed from the hand of the enemy,"
Psalm 107:2

Ransomed: Let the redeemed of the LORD say so...

First Edition

International Standard Book Number:
1-59196-511- X

In Memory
Of
Richard H. and Juliette V. Whittemore

Acknowledgments

There are so many fine people who the Lord brought into my life after my attempted suicide that these words will never express the gratitude that I have for them. I wish I could name everyone, but I believe that would be another book in itself. In fact, I debated whether or not to include this page because I was afraid of offending someone I should have recognized. However, not to mention even a few would be unacceptable at the very least. If I have left you out, I know our God has much more of a treasure awaiting you then my mere words.

First and foremost, I want to thank my Lord and Savior Jesus Christ. He met me where I was at and lifted me out of that pit of despair and into His Glorious Light, thus reconciling me to our Father in Heaven. Halleluyah!!! And He has been faithful ever since. How could this speck of dust adequately thank so Great a God as ours? The closest I can come is, "I thank You, my Dear Holy Father, for my life in You, which You restored through Jesus. And it is in His Wonderful Name I thank You and praise You. Amen."

To my father and mother, Richard and Juliette Whittemore, I dedicate this book. My reasons are twofold. First, my mother's seed of salvation finally took root, and second because my dad inspired me to write this testimony. This inspiration came through the reading of his book, "Look to This Day," which came into my knowledge and possession long after his death.

Certainly my words are not enough to express my appreciation and thankfulness to Ginny, who was my wife at the time and who stayed with me during some very difficult years after my suicide attempt. She not only kept her job and kept our family together but also arranged for some seventeen surgeries to reconstruct my face. I am sorry I was not there for her when she went through her own difficult times battling cancer afterward. Thank God that is behind her now and she is healed by His mercies. I hope and pray we remain good friends at the very least.

Many thanks to my sister Laurie for also encouraging me to write this book and then helped me with how to publish it. She continually gave me tips on writing and then cheered me on when I finally got started.

And to my wonderful children who accepted their prodigal dad back without condition, I am eternally thankful. Suzette, Bill, Brian, Stephanie, Julie, and Melissa, as well as my ten grandchildren, are a blessing in my life that I do not deserve. My quiver is full. Oh, how my Lord gives me what I do not deserve and does not give me what I do!

Millie Stamm and Larry Girtin came to my aid from different directions and families and provided the framework for my spiritual healing while many whom Millie and Larry knew, I am sure, kept us in much-needed prayer. This is also in light of the fact they did not even know my family or me prior to my attempted suicide. They were sent by God to minister to us, and now they are enjoying their just rewards in heaven for their faithfulness to Him throughout their lives. "Well done, good and faithful servants," is what I am sure they heard Jesus say when they arrived in His court.

Then there are two unnamed "angels," one who found me on the ground and called the helicopter to carry me to the hospital. The second was the emergency medical doctor who first attended me at St. Joseph's Hospital. In those first few minutes, their swift and professional actions were keys to my survival.

Also the crew of the "Life Flight" helicopter that ferried me to the hospital, pilot Denny Fox, flight nurse Randy Clowdus, and paramedic Jeff Mize, were exceptional professionals. Randy and Jeff encouraged me during the flight, and later they all visited me to see how I was doing. They truly acted beyond the call of duty.

The many doctors and nurses who attended me were certainly sent by God to put my body and mind back together. They spent many hours on my case sometimes calling and visiting me on their own time. Thank you Drs. Barnthouse, Clark, Faerber, Goodman, Manson, Sternberg, and Van Blarcome. You will never know the impact you have had on my life. Also, there were two nurses, Phyllis Azman and Judy Rollings, who spent many hours assisting the doctors on my behalf. Thank you for the special attention and encouragement you gave to me.

And thank you, Frances Weisbein, for the many Bible studies at your home during my recovery. Your prayers and insightfulness provided much healing for my soul.

Last but not least by any measure, I thank Faye Stockwell, mother of our four children, Suzette, Bill, Brian, and Julie, who kept praying for our salvation over many years. And Wells, Faye's husband, for being the father I wasn't. The Lord heard Faye's prayer and answered her in a very powerful way on December 27, 1998, when all four children, three of their spouses, our oldest grandchild, and me were all baptized together—in Faye's church!

Ransomed: Let the redeemed of the LORD say so...

Contents

INTRODUCTION

What is truth? That is the question Pontius Pilate posed to Jesus when He was brought before him to be condemned and sentenced to death. Pilate was staring Truth right in the face and didn't want to accept it, because of the angry mob waiting outside to crucify Jesus.

In some ways, not much has changed since that day. Many still want to silence Jesus. We have taken prayer out of our schools, tolerate lifestyles that were never condoned by God, and now we are even in the process of tearing down any reminders of our Law Giver from our buildings and institutions once founded on those very laws, the Ten Commandments.

I know because I was part of that angry crowd outside for many years, believing, Who needs a Savior when I can do it all myself? This story begins with how doing it "my way" most of my life, as the old Frank Sinatra song goes, leads to death. But by the grace of God, I was blessed to be born again and let God through Jesus show me the only way to Truth and to do it His way. So this story is about a loving and merciful God who wants none to perish but all to come to repentance and Salvation.

I know there is no way for me to convince anyone of the Truth, because God is the only One who can change hearts. But what I hope and pray is that through what you read in this book, if you haven't committed your heart to God, this will encourage you to ask God to show you the Truth Himself. And when you do, I promise you He will show you the Truth, and it will set you free, ransoming you also from the penalty of death.

I hope you will also see that this story is about a loving God's amazing grace and mercy that will help anyone who will call on His Name. I also hope and pray this story will further encourage you and give you the assurance that the faith and hope you place in our Lord Jesus Christ will lift you up "*on wings as eagles*" above any circumstance. And that He will never leave us or forsake us as long as we obey Him, because He has "ransomed" us to be with Him for all eternity.

Paul, in Romans 8:28, said it best: *"And we know that all things work together for good to those who love God, to those who are the called according to His purpose."*

CHAPTER ONE

THE PIT

Psalm 18:5
The cords of the grave coiled around me;
the snares of death confronted me.
(NIV)

Psalm 34:6
This poor man cried out, and the LORD heard him,
And saved him out of all his troubles.

For a change it was not a busy morning. I had completed some administrative paper work and got up to look out of my office window which overlooked the street below. As an executive in a large corporation in charge of some five hundred people, responsible for a $150 million dollar budget and bringing home a nice six-figure salary, what more could I want? Oh yes, I was married for the third time to a beautiful woman and had a wonderful daughter, but everyone has been married before, so what's the big deal. In today's world, one might say I was successful.

Yet this day I realized something was missing. As I looked out the window and reviewed how I got to this position, I thought to myself, Is this all there is? Three months later I was without a job.

It was during the terrible recession of 1990. Many executives lost their jobs because of downsizing by major corporations, and I was certainly not unique in that situation. But it hit me doubly hard because I had made my career my god. I was defined by my job. After all, hadn't I sacrificed marriages, children, and friends, everything for

that god? And now it was gone. Just like that—over, done. I felt I had nothing and no one I could depend on.
The next year and a half, I kept sinking deeper and deeper into depression (see Appendix A, Depression: What Is It?).

Some friends who were terminated with me and I started a consulting business, but it became more difficult for me just to concentrate, let alone work. It was like being trapped in a funnel where I felt myself sinking but the smooth sides prevented me from stopping the fall. No one around me could tell the agony I was in. I kept it all inside, never sharing with my wife, Ginny, or with anyone else that I was out of control. I was used to being in charge, so I thought I could lick this.

When depression goes untreated, one loses the ability to reach out for help. However, it is very treatable, and some eighty percent who suffer from it can be treated successfully. But because I lacked the ability now to seek and get help, thoughts of suicide started to occupy my mind as a way to end this misery. A negative kind of logic set in, and I could rationalize in my own mind that not only was suicide the only way to end this life in the pit but it would be better for my family as well.

I must mention here that losing a position and all the benefits associated with it should not, by itself, be enough to sink one into such a state. But for me, it was at the very least a contributing factor and at the most a catalyst, but it was not the cause. No, the cause had many contributing factors. I won't go into them all for very personal reasons, but the major contributing factor was my lifestyle. I had been a heavy drinker, a closet alcoholic with the corresponding relationships to go with it. Three marriages were one consequence of this lifestyle. Although I drank much less during my third marriage, the damage had been done to my system, and the drinking played a deadly role in my hitting bottom, as you will soon see.

I hit the bottom of the pit on January 27, 1992, the day after the Super Bowl. I remember this because the day of the Super Bowl we had a little party and I had a few drinks. I remember thinking how drinking didn't pick me up anymore but seemed to drag me down. By the end of the game, I felt as though I had hit bottom, the lowest point I have ever been in my life, as though I couldn't go any lower. That was it. I couldn't take it anymore. The decision was made, so I put the gun in the car that night without my wife noticing and went to bed.

Some people with depression have a hard time sleeping, but for some reason I didn't. What I remember about my sleep while depressed was that it was a black sleep. It was as if I was in a dark cave, no light and no dreams, no REM sleep at all. Getting up was always hard, and it was tough to get going in the morning. I just didn't want to face the day. It was having a terrible effect on our marriage too, because I had no desire for intimacy.

The next morning when I got up, I felt no better. Ginny had gone to work, and our nanny was caring for our daughter, Melissa. I wrote a note, kissed Melissa good-bye, and headed for a secluded place that I had in mind. After parking the car at approximately 11:35 a.m., I took out the gun and put the barrel under my chin. As I had my finger on the trigger, it was if I could hear a voice say, "Go ahead and do it. You have never done anything right in your life anyway." But then a cry for help came out of me, like no other cry before, as I asked God's forgiveness.

My cry to God did not keep me from pulling the trigger, but as I now know from God's Word, the Bible, *"Whoever calls on the name of the LORD shall be saved"* (Joel 2:32; Romans 10:13). By a miracle I was alive and knew this was not the way to handle my problems. In that split second, God kept the bullet from killing me. I staggered out of the car and fell to the ground. When I lay on my side, I could breathe, but when I rolled onto my back, I was drowning in my own blood.

As I look back, God seemed to be saying, "Do you want to live or die?" I rolled onto my side. I wanted to live. It was almost immediately that God sent me help. What a forgiving and merciful God we have.

CHAPTER TWO

REDEEMED

Psalm 116:6,8
The LORD preserves the simple;
I was brought low, and He saved me.
...For You have delivered my soul from death,
My eyes from tears,
And my feet from falling.

Before I knew it, a woman found me. Then almost immediately it seemed, a helicopter ambulance evacuated me to a hospital. Randy and Jeff, the flight nurse and paramedic comforted me and encouraged me to hang on. They put a trachea tube into my throat almost immediately. From this point on, the Lord started surrounding me with the most beautiful professionals and others that ministered to me and brought healing to my body, soul and spirit. And yes, some were angels.

At some point during that flight to the hospital, I lost consciousness. I don't remember much except slivers of time during the next two weeks. There was a trauma nurse named Judy Rollings who was in the emergency room when I came in. She stayed with me, giving me encouragement, and she continued to do so during my month's stay there. Afterward, she remained a good friend, helping me with my volunteer work at the same hospital.

Miraculously, there were two specialists, Drs. Barnthouse and Faerber, on duty at the hospital when I arrived, and they worked on me almost immediately. Dr. Barnthouse was a plastic surgeon and Dr. Faerber a maxillofacial surgeon. It was because of their quick work that much of the tissue in my face, which was completely blown apart, was saved.

Ginny arrived with a friend shortly after I was admitted. She, of course, was in complete shock, having no clue how this could have happened. She was wondering what had brought her world tumbling down around her. It so traumatized Ginny that for a few years after my suicide attempt, she could not drive on the interstate highways without an anxiety attack.

Ginny did all she could to help me. She set up the specialists who would operate to repair a face they had never seen before and that was so badly damaged it took seventeen-plus surgeries to get it in functional order. Plus she kept a house in order, worked, and cared for our daughter, Melissa. I will always be grateful for how she hung in there with me for those first few years after that fateful day. I can only imagine how difficult it was for her. And I was not much help during that time. Unfortunately, our marriage ended in August of 1998. Ginny and Melissa are constantly in my prayers, and I know Ginny's reward will be with the Lord someday.

As I've mentioned, the Lord brought many fine people to help me climb back into life, many whom I had never met before. His timing was always perfect. Because I didn't know the Lord in a personal way, He would bring people into my life and work through them as He drew me nearer to Him.

In the first days out of intensive care, Perry Turner, a friend from work, came to see me almost every day—just to be with me. What a blessing Perry was during those early days, because other than Ginny, he was my only consistent visitor. I know now what it means just to be with someone who is having a hard time. Just being there means more than talking, because sometimes you don't want to talk or even know what to say. And I couldn't have talked if I had wanted to because of the trachea tube in my throat.

Many family members and friends wrote to me and sent cards, and these were uplifting as well.

One of my favorite stories in the Bible (John 4:1–26) is about the Samaritan woman Jesus met by the well in Schechem (now Neblus), a town in Samaria. Jews of that day would not go there, because the Samaritans, Israelites who had intermarried with people of other cultures, were a despised people. It was noon, the hot part of the day when the women usually would not go to the well, but this one woman did because she was despised even by her own people. She was a woman who had been married five times and now was living with a man. Jesus asked her for a drink of water, and in their conversation, she became aware that He was more than a prophet, that, in fact, He was the Messiah, the Anointed One. She ran to tell the town's people to come out and meet Him, and they, too, realized He was the Messiah.

It is absolutely amazing, but I am coming to understand what our God will do for everyone. For the Samaritan women, God Almighty put on the flesh of a man, came down from His throne in heaven to meet her right where she was at, and saved her. This is exactly what Jesus did for me. He met me at the bottom of the well and saved me. And He does this for all of us. Even I as try to understand this unconditional love God has for each one of us, it is still hard for me to grasp.

In those early days, it was if I was just starting to climb out of a well. I could look up and see a light, but I knew I was still in the well. It would be a while before I realized that the light was the Lord and He was bringing me toward Him. He had redeemed me!

CHAPTER THREE

THE TAPESTRY OF HOPE

Daniel 2:22
He reveals deep and secret things;
He knows what is in the darkness,
And light dwells with Him.

Sometime during the two weeks I was in intensive care, I had three visions. They were life-changing experiences for me, and they started me on the path to receive God in my life through Jesus Christ. After my attempt at suicide and the dramatic way the Lord God saved me, it does not take a rocket scientist to realize that "my way" was not the way of life God had created me for.

In the first vision, I was before a tapestry, a white sheet with gold inlaid squares, which filled my whole field of vision. In all but one square, there was black writing with varying numbers of lines in each. I could not read what was written, because I did not recognize the alphabet used. Today I know it was Hebrew.

There were two angels there with me, and it seemed they communicated to me at the same time, saying that I could gaze upon this tapestry as long as I liked. It was cool but not cold on my face there and very peaceful. As I looked at this brilliant white sheet with its gold squares, I could see that the top left square had one line of writing in it; and in the center, there was a square that was full of writing. But the bottom right-hand square was empty; there was no writing in it.

For one short moment as I gazed on this beautiful tapestry, I had the sensation of standing behind myself, but it did not last long. Finally I said, not verbally, but in something like intuitive communication, "What is this?" They answered by saying, "It is all the good things you have done in your lives." Lives? This puzzled me for sometime until I came to realize later that when I accepted Christ into my life I became a "*new creation*" (2 Corinthians 5:17). Therefore, my old self died that day and now I am "*born again*" into a new life in Christ.

As my time in this wonderful place was drawing to a close, the two angels pointed to the empty square and said, "You have to go back and fill this in."

The vision ended then but has stayed with me as a constant reminder of how real God is in my life, and that He cares more than I know how to comprehend and then love like He loves us.

For a long time I thought that filling in that empty square in the tapestry was something I had to do, some mission some special assignment. But I have come to understand that it was not so much "doing" as it was in coming into a personal relationship with God. After all, He has said in His Word, He is *the God of Abraham, the God of Isaac, and the God of Jacob.* He is the God of individuals. That is the way He created us. And it is the way He wants to relate to us. And that way, I have found, is through Jesus.

Why Jesus? I hope that during the course of this book, God will reveal that truth to you. But for now, suffice it to say that God loves us so much that He wants none of us to perish but to turn from our wrong ways of doing things and let Him show us the right way. If it were just a matter of doing good deeds, then I wouldn't have had to come back. I had a tapestry full them. No, the Lord wanted me to come back, come to know Him, be reconciled to Him through Jesus, and help others find this Truth, too. This, I believe, is my main mission.

God showed us very early in the Bible that He wanted a personal relationship with us. Soon after He created this world and Adam and Eve to live in it (Genesis 1 and 2), He created the institution of marriage. He said, *"Therefore a man shall leave his father and mother and be joined to his wife, and they shall become one flesh"* (Genesis 2:24). God created this institution for men and women because, I believe, it is the kind of relationship He wants to have with us—that personal, that intimate, that close. Verse 25 is just as important, I think, because He tells us He wants our relationship with Him to be totally open, hiding nothing. *"And they were both naked, the man and his wife, and were not ashamed."*

Jesus drove this point home when just before He was crucified, He prayed *"that they all may be one, as You, Father, are in Me, and I in You; that they also may be one in Us, that the world may believe that You sent Me"* (John 17:21).

Certainly one of the most powerful and important meanings I have received from the vision of the Tapestry of Hope is that once God forgives our sins, He remembers them no more. As I discovered later, Scripture tells us this, too. In Psalm 103:12, David tells us, "*As far as the east is from the west, So far has He removed our transgressions from us."* In Isaiah 43:25, we are reminded, *"I, even I, am He who blots out your transgressions for My own sake; And I will not remember your sins."* And Jeremiah 31:34, speaking of the New Covenant, which the Lord Jesus would pay with His life for us to have, says, *"I will forgive their inequity, and their sin I will remember no more."* This "New Covenant" that Jesus brings us (Luke 22:20) and His forgiveness doesn't abolish the laws God originally gave us on tablets of stone, representing hearts of stone I believe. But because His laws will be written on our hearts of flesh (Jeremiah 31:33), we will have the will to obey God by the power of the Holy Spirit working in us to separate us from sin (John 14:16). This will make the old way "*obsolete*" (Hebrews 8:13), trying to obey God in our own strength, when this process is complete.

We all can have this forgiveness because God, knowing we can't save ourselves from the temptations of this world, came to earth and put on the skin of man so He could die in our place. He took our sins upon Him that we might enjoy eternal life with our Father in heaven. As the angel of the Lord told Joseph about the Son his soon-to-be wife, Mary, was carrying, *"And she will bring forth a Son, and you shall call His name JESUS, for He will save His people from their sins"* (Matthew 1:21). Aren't these great promises? And I saw this confirmed in my tapestry—only the good deeds were written down; there were no sins recorded! Praise God!!!

But as I mentioned before, if only good deeds were needed to enter heaven, then I would not have had to return to fill in that last square. Think about it. Picture yourself walking up to any house; knocking on the door; and when the man of the house answers, you say, "I am going to live here now because I am a good person." Do you think that would get you in? Of course not! And this is why God so desperately wants a personal relationship with us—so we can know Him, not just about Him.

Now picture that you are knocking on Heaven's door; this time God answers the door, and you tell Him, "Well, I've done all these good things, so now I am coming in to live with You for all eternity even though I don't know You." Does that make any sense? However, God gives us a way to know Him in a very personal way through His son, Jesus. And He is *"the way, the truth and the life,"* the only way. Why is Jesus the only way? We will discuss this more later, but if God didn't provide the way, how would we ever know the *true* way?

The vision of the Tapestry of Hope has stayed with me in a very vivid and comforting way and gives me much peace, especially when sharing it with others. Since that encounter, I have the strongest need to tell of my experience by the saving grace of our loving Redeemer. And our Lord has given me the opportunity to share it in situations that only He initiates. I'll share some of those experiences later in this book.

CHAPTER FOUR

THE DARK SIDE

Psalm 55:4
My heart is severely pained within me,
And the terrors of death have fallen upon me.

Ephesians 2:12
that at that time you were without Christ,
being aliens from the commonwealth of Israel
and strangers from the covenants of promise,
having no hope and without God in the world.

The above two verses sum up in a very real sense the second and third visions I experienced after the Tapestry of Hope. In these next two visions, God was clearly showing me what it would be like to be without Him for all eternity. These two visions also occurred while I was still in intensive care in the hospital.

In the second vision, I was led into a very dark area. I could not see anything except a being in red. It was if I was going to be shown around when all of a sudden, angry voices told the being who was leading me that I wasn't staying there. Then the vision ended.

There was a sense of nothing there, and I wondered about the angry voices. I felt rejected and hurt by them. After all, I was just being shown around. It puzzled me until I gained the full significance of the third vision.

In the third vision, which seemed to occur shortly after the second one, I was in a battle for my life and I seemed to be holding my own. I was battling things—and they were things—I don't know how else to describe them. It was like something out of a horror movie. Then this giant hideous creature started to attack me. And as it got closer, it got larger until it seemed to engulf me.

The only way I can give you any sense of the terror that possessed me at this point is to ask you to remember the most frightening nightmare you have ever had. Now couple that with the feeling that you know you are having a nightmare, but you can't wake up. That is something like this vision, only worse. It was a few years later when I was reading the Book of Daniel that I came upon the following verse and immediately felt it was describing the beast I had experienced in my vision.

"After this I saw in the night visions, and behold, a fourth beast, dreadful and terrible, exceedingly strong. It had huge iron teeth; it was devouring, breaking in pieces, and trampling the residue with its feet. It was different from all the beasts that were before it, and it had ten horns." (Daniel 7:7)

As this beast approached me, I knew there was nothing I could do to stop him from overpowering me. At that point, I cried out to God for help. In an instant, this thing that was about to consume me turned into water droplets and disappeared. This whole scene just collapsed right before my eyes.

The sense of relief I had at that moment was like I could breathe again. I had life. It is hard to describe. That was the beginning, I believe, of realizing God is real and I can call on Him to help me. It also instilled in me that I never wanted to be without God again. The place I was in with those creatures was a place without God. It was a horrible existence. It was hell, and it further convinced me to want to know this God who redeemed me *"from the hand of the enemy."*

As I came through this vapor, I found myself looking at a nurse standing at the foot of my bed. This became my first clear memory of being in the hospital. The nurse said to me, "We are taking you out of intensive care." It had now been about two weeks since my Lord and Savior miraculously saved me from death.

It was also the start of a long road to recovery with many difficult days ahead. But the major difference I had in facing difficulties this time was that I had God, who—I was beginning to realize—would *"never leave me or forsake me."*

CHAPTER FIVE

TRANSFORMATION

Philippians 2:12-13
Therefore, my beloved, as you have always obeyed, not as in my presence only, but now much more in my absence, work out your own salvation with fear and trembling; for it is God who works in you both to will and to do for His good pleasure.

It was after I was taken out of intensive care and put in a regular ward and was able to get around on my own that I started to see changes taking place in me. I had an overwhelming sense of contrition and desire to get right with God. I remember taking my first shower and sobbing under the water telling the Lord how sorry I was for everything I had done wrong and asking Him for forgiveness. *"For godly sorrow produces repentance leading to salvation, not to be regretted; but the sorrow of the world produces death"* (2 Corinthians 7:10).

What I would learn in this process is that once God forgives, He remembers our sins no more (Isaiah 43:25). But I still remembered them, and the guilt I felt was overwhelming. It would be some time before I understood that this feeling of guilt was not coming from God but from the enemy, the devil, who hates to loose the battle for our souls and will do everything, once we are saved, to try to convince us that we are not saved.

I give thanks that the Lord God gives us His Holy Spirit to work in us *"to will and to do for His good purpose."* Unfortunately, this Power given to us is not stressed enough in Christian teachings, leaving many to think they are on their own when working out their *own salvation with fear and trembling*. What we are "working out" is not a matter of earning salvation. We already have that gift. But when we submit our wills to our Lord, He will transform us into the image of Jesus (Philippians 3:20–21). This means letting the Holy Spirit have the power over our flesh to sanctify us (separate us) from sin, thereby replacing our desire to sin with the desire to obey God. This includes removing those things from our lives that can influence us and lead us to sin (*"lead us not into temptation"*).

This change in desire came about in several ways. For example, one of the first treatments I received was being placed into a hyperbaric chamber where oxygen was piped in until the pressure was equal to being under the water at about thirty-five feet. Although this treatment was somewhat controversial in the medical profession, when I was treated in 1992, it seemed to work well for healing my type of injury. It is believed to accelerate healing in tissue, and since much of my face was damaged, this was the treatment recommended.

There was a TV/VCR set up outside the chamber, but I had no control over it once I was inside the chamber. As they were placing me into the chamber, the nurse asked me if I wanted to see a Robin Hood movie, and I said OK. I had always enjoyed action movies and what I had termed "blood and guts" movies, the more blood the better. However, as the movie played and the violence and fighting started, I could feel within my spirit a revulsion of these scenes that were now being played out in front on me. It was at that moment I realized something was changing within me. I didn't understand it, but I knew I didn't want to see or even condone this type of violence again.

Eventually I lost my desire to see or want anything do with other things I used to enjoy and condone, such as unfit television & movies, sexual immorality, drinking (I was an alcoholic), swearing and I had even tried marijuana. Later, for example, I was at a movie that contained such fowl language that I got up and walked out because it grieved my spirit so. Today I do not go to a movie unless I feel comfortable that it would not offend God, so, needless to say, I hardly ever go to a movie. I'm much the same about TV except for tuning on the news from time to time. But even the news has its drawbacks with its slanted secular views on events in our world and its constant appetite for anything violent or sexual to report on.

Looking back, I can see that the Lord first addressed those areas in my life that had influence on me and that He gave me the will not to indulge in them anymore. However, along with the behavior change that God was working in my life, a sense of self-righteousness crept in. It was if now "I" knew the "way" and "I" was going to save everyone in my family. Unfortunately, this self-righteous attitude was the straw that broke the camel's back, I believe, in my marriage to Ginny. As she told me later, "You are not the man that I married," and she was absolutely right. In those very difficult days, I remember praying, "Lord, if I am in the way of Ginny's salvation, then please get me out of the way." After our divorce in 1998, I thought about that prayer and have wondered if I had prayed, "Lord please save this marriage," what the outcome would have been. In any case, I am sorry for the failure on my part that contributed to yet another failed marriage. But on a happy note, I have just received word from Ginny that she is going to be married in 2004, and I am glad for the joy that is returning to her and our daughter's lives.

Other areas of my life that were not right with God took longer to change, only because I would not let go of them right away. Thank God for His patience with me. For example, I used to love to gamble, and at the time, I didn't believe it affected anyone but me. But as the Holy Spirit started to convict me that this behavior grieved Him, the fleshly desire in me started to fight back. I remember rationalizing—never try to rationalize with God, because you will loose every time—Well, I won't gamble in the United States anymore, because someone I know might see me. But if I gamble where no one knows me, I am just affecting myself. Right? Wrong! As I have learned, someone is always watching us, and our behavior is a testimony of whether we are partnering with God in our lives or not.

In a rare time that Ginny and I were able to get away by ourselves after my attempted suicide, we went to the Bahamas for a short vacation. Of course, I headed for the casino and some blackjack, which I thought I loved to play. However, this time I was not enjoying it even though I was winning. I could not put my finger on the reason, but somehow I felt it was not right. After we had returned to the states, I was driving our car and listening to a Christian radio station, where I heard Pastor Tony Evans preaching on why gambling is a sin. Tony used the playing of lotto, which I had also enjoyed, as an example of why gambling is a sin and of how gambling negatively effects others.

In his example, Tony explained that many people who play lotto are poor, and a winner is taking money from them. When we condone this practice, we were drawing others into to it, especially those with the most to loose. That sermon convicted me on the spot, and soon afterward my gambling days ended.

Someone reading this might ask, "You mean when we accept Jesus into our lives we have to give up all the fun things of life?" First, what I have learned is that this life is not about me, it is about my Savior, who died for me that I may live with Him in glory for all eternity. Second, this life is temporary. We are just sojourners here being refined like silver and gold, getting the "dross" removed—that stuff in our lives that gets between God and us. Like my career, for example, that so consumed me that I sacrificed the good things of this life, God, family and friends for it. If we never come to this realization, we are just living our lives for "things." Jesus said, *"For what profit is it to a man if he gains the whole world, and loses his own soul? Or what will a man give in exchange for his soul?"* (Matthew 16:26).

This transformation included separating me from a sinful behavior (a process which will continue, thankfully, since I am not there yet). As Paul said in Philippians 1:6, *"Being confident of this very thing, that He who has begun a good work in you will complete it until the day of Jesus Christ."*

Reconciliation

The Lord also gave me the desire to repair and reconcile as best I could those relationships that I had destroyed (2 Corinthians 5:18), to tell those I hurt that I am sorry, and to seek their forgiveness. So for two years, mostly in the summer months, I traveled around the country in an RV (my home at that time), visiting my children and seeing my first two wives in the process. This has been a difficult process on one hand but very rewarding on the other.

On the difficult side, it would be nice to report that I have been reconciled to all my family and friends and that all is well. Unfortunately, that is not the case. For example, I still have a daughter, as of this writing, who will not see me or even talk with me. However, I know that our Lord is in charge of all our situations, and I will continue to pray for our reconciliation and for whatever changes that are needed in us to bring us together again.

From my experience in reconciliation and forgiveness, I have learned that unlike Divine forgiveness, where we are always reconciled to our Father in heaven through Jesus, there is not always reconciliation with human forgiveness. This is because of the hurt that remains and may remain for the rest of our life. This hurt, however, must not be confused with not forgiving someone of his or her wrong against us. I believe the Good Lord allows hurt as a reminder to keep us from doing hurtful things to others and also to help us build better relationships in the future while maintaining the ones we still have.

In the Bible, Jacob and Esau are a good example of this human characteristic of forgiving and reconciling (Genesis 25–36). Jacob conned his brother Esau into giving away his birthright, but later in their lives, he sought reconciliation. However, even though Esau forgave his brother, they did not associate with each other again. But Jacob went on to be the great patriarch of the Israelites. Esau went on to establish Edom, which is Jordan today. Even though there is peace between Israel and Jordan at this time, there is certainly no spirit of reconciliation between them.

The rewarding part came slowly but with ever-increasing intensity as the Lord worked powerfully in our lives, bringing my children and me together and healing old wounds within family and friends; a process that continues today. As the psalmist says, *"He heals the brokenhearted and binds up their wounds. Great is our Lord, and mighty in power; His understanding is infinite"* (Psalm 147:3,5).

One day while I was visiting my dear daughter Julie and her wonderful family, she said to me, "Dad, Bill [her brother] and I were talking, and we think we should get baptized. What do you think?" I had thought about baptism and was even thinking about being baptized in the river Jordan in Israel during an upcoming trip I was planning, but it was beyond my wildest dreams that we could all be baptized together. Little did I know at the time that their mother, Faye, had continued to pray over these many years for our salvation, and the Lord was about to answer her prayer in a very powerful way.

About a year later, as only the Lord could arrange, I was again at my daughter Julie's for Christmas. My dear daughter Sue and her beautiful family were flying in from Oregon. My dear sons, Bill and Brian, and their wonderful families were driving to Pennsylvania to meet up with everyone at their mother's and step dad's, Faye and Wells', home. They were so gracious to include me in this wonderful gathering. It was the first time in twenty-eight years that all of us would be together for Christmas. What a Christmas it would be, as our baptisms were scheduled for two days later.

However, because Bill's wife Laura's parents lived in Ohio, they had planned to be with us only during Christmas Eve, and then they would drive to Ohio to spend Christmas Day with her parents. That would mean they would not be baptized with us. But the Lord is always in charge, and I have learned we can always trust in Him, even when situations seem impossible.

Two days before Christmas we received a call from Sue that they were stranded in Denver because of bad weather. It meant it would be late Christmas Eve before they could fly into Cleveland, near Bill's home and where I was staying at the time. We would pick them up at the airport and then all drive to Faye and Well's for our Christmas celebration.

This put a crimp in Bill and Laura's plans because it would mean they would have hardly any time to visit with Sue and Jeff or time for the cousins to play together. However, the Lord used this circumstance to further heal our wounds and bring praise and glory to God through His Son, whose birthday we were about to celebrate.

That night before Sue and Jeff and their boys arrived, Bill and I stayed up until 3 a.m. discussing the past and the hurt from my actions that Bill still carried with him. We were able to get a lot out in the open and allow the Lord to start the healing process. Then later that morning, they told me they were changing their plans and would spend Christmas Eve with Laura's parents and Christmas with the rest of us...and they would join us to be baptized, too. Halleluyah!!!

It is hard for me to put appropriate words to this exceptionally wonderful time we spent together that Christmas. But as if to put an exclamation point to Faye's faithful prayers for her family and me, the Lord gathered us all together two days later to be baptized. In a small church in Faye's hometown, our four children, Sue, Bill, Brian, and Julie; three of their spouses, Jeff, Laura, and Nancy: and our oldest grandson, Brandon, who is Sue and Jeff's son, and me we were all baptized together—in Faye's own church where she was baptized at age thirteen!

What a testimony of God's faithfulness to His promises! Here we were, all gathered together in answer to Faye's prayers for our salvation and then baptized in the church she attends and was baptized in herself! Only an Awesome, Wonderful, Merciful, and Loving God could make all that happen in such a powerful way. It is also a testimony about never giving up, for our Lord is faithful and true and as Jesus said, *"Ask, and it will be given to you; seek, and you will find; knock, and it will be opened to you"* (Matthew 7:7). (An easy way to remember this verse when you may want to call upon it for comfort in the future is to remember the word **ASK**: **A**sk, **S**eek, and **K**nock.)

God Speaks Through Children

In my travels I started to learn the way God would speak to me. I discovered He speaks to us through His Word, the Bible; through other people; and through our circumstances. But one of the clearest ways He communicates with me is through the small children in my life, as I learned with my grandson Brian.

One day while I was out visiting Sue and her delightful family in Oregon, I had taken her oldest son, Brandon, to school with his then 2-year-old brother, Brian. After we walked Brandon to his class, Brian and I went out into the schoolyard to play in the playground. There was a tunnel he loved to crawl through, which led to a ladder that he would climb up and then go down the slide. Every time Brian would get halfway up this ladder, he would stop look, over at me, and say, "Help, Grandpa." So I would touch his back with my hand to reassure him that he wouldn't fall backward; then he would climb the rest of the way up the ladder on his own.

After Brian climbed the ladder and said "Help, Grandpa" a few times, I said to him, "You know who really helps us, don't you?" He replied, "Jesus," and then climbed the rest of the way up the ladder. When he got to the top, he turned around, looked down at me, and said with all the authority and wisdom of someone much older than his 2 years, "Jesus is alive!"

Later when I was sharing this precious moment with Sue, she said quite matter-of-factly, "Oh, I hear Brian talk to Jesus when he is out on the porch." No wonder Jesus said, *"Let the little children come to me, and do not forbid them for such is the kingdom of heaven"* (Matthew 19:14). And as it also says in God's Word, *"Out of the mouth of babes and nursing infants You have ordained strength, Because of Your enemies, That You may silence the enemy and the avenger"* (Psalm 8:2). May we hear You speak more often, Dear Lord, through our children.

Brian's older brother, Brandon, has taken what he is learning about the Lord from Sue and Jeff and is already letting the Lord's light and his love for the Lord shine through him to others. Sue shared this with me recently, a testimony of this wonderful boy's unselfishness.

Brandon is an exceptional athlete like his dad and has helped lead his teams in basketball and football (under Jeff's coaching) to their city's championships. This year was no exception in football. Brandon's team, where this year he shared quarterbacking duties with another boy, was playing the only team that they had lost to during the regular season. It was a very tight championship game, and at halftime, and when they would usually switch quarterbacks, Jeff felt he couldn't afford to let Brandon take his rotation, because he wasn't warmed up and loose for his turn. Their team went on to win this championship game 7 to 6 without Brandon quarterbacking.

After the celebration, Sue and Jeff stayed until after everyone else had left to see if they could help clean up. The lights were still on the field when Jeff approached the man in charge of the field to see what they could do. While the men were talking, Sue turned to see Brandon in the middle of that lighted field on his knees with his hands raised to heaven, thanking Jesus.

I am sure Brandon was very disappointed that he didn't get to play in that championship game but I couldn't help but be grateful and proud that his first priority was thanking God for the victory. In imagining Brandon returning to the field of play to thank Jesus reminded me of the one leper that returned to thank Jesus for making him well. *"So Jesus answered and said, 'Were there not ten cleansed? But where are the nine? Were there not any found who returned to give glory to God except this foreigner?' And He said to him, 'Arise, go your way. Your faith has made you well'"* (Luke 17:17–19). Brandon was certainly made well in his faith that day.

Suffering

Another powerful lesson the Lord taught me was about suffering, and this time He used my grandson Xavier, my daughter Julie's and her husband Keith's oldest son. But first I would like to comment on what I believe to be at least three reasons for suffering in this life: (1) our sin, (2) the benefit of others, (3) our growth.

First, suffering comes as a result of our sin, our wrong choices (John 5:14). It is true Jesus paid the penalty for our sins; however, we must face the consequences of our choices. Everything we do affects someone in our life, from our good choices to our bad ones. Someone is always watching us

I was reminded of consequences in a good way in late 2002 when I was taking a bus from Jerusalem to Ashqelon. Because I was a part-time bus driver at the time, I was really impressed at how the driver handled his bus. He drove it so smoothly that you knew he had the comfort of his passengers in mind. As I got off the bus, I told him as best I could in Hebrew what a good job he had done and that I was a bus driver in America. He thanked me—in English! Well, a few weeks later as I was waiting for a bus in Ashqelon, a young woman approached me and said she was on that bus that day when I complimented the bus driver. She thought it was a nice thing to do and thanked me. I am using this example, not for my glory, but as an example of good choices and their effects. And, admittedly,

it is much more gratifying to talk about right choices than wrong choices and their consequences. I have already described the suffering I experienced as the result of the latter; for example, my family and I experienced suffering as a consequence of the sin in my life; by me making those bad choices that led to broken marriages, children without their father and much more. Eventually that lifestyle contributed to my depression and resulting suicide attempt.

Second, suffering in our lives may have nothing to do with us but everything to do with the workings of God to reach others through us. When my daughter Melissa was in kindergarten, there was a disadvantaged boy in her class, and her school did not place disadvantaged students in a separate class, which I think most of the parents supported wholeheartedly. It allowed the other students to bring these "special" children along with them, so to speak. And the love for this particular boy that developed among his classmates was like a magnet, pulling them into the common cause of helping him. It was beautiful to watch this loving interaction among these children. Certainly the love of Christ was displayed in their young lives, and it was felt by us as parents as well.

In John 9, Jesus healed a blind man who was suffering for a greater purpose and not as a consequence of sin. When He was asked if this man had been blind since birth because of his sin or the sin of his parents, Jesus answered, *"Neither this man nor his parents sinned, but that the works of God should be revealed in him"* (John 9:3).

Third, I believe we suffer because from suffering we learn to persevere, and through perseverance we grow, we build character (Romans 5:3–4), and find our Lord and His compassion and mercy. As James said in his epistle, *"Indeed we count them blessed who endure. You have heard of the perseverance of Job and seen the end intended by the Lord—that the Lord is very compassionate and merciful"* (James 5:11). It was my suffering with depression (also as a consequence of the lifestyle I had chosen) that led to the suicide attempt. But it was my Lord and Savior who patiently waited for me to reach the end of my strength and finally turn to Him (my choice) so He could help me. If we honestly look at our sufferings, we can see the things we have learned from them and the growth in our lives that has resulted from them.

The story of Job is a great example of this kind of suffering, and like every other story in the Bible, it is included for our edification and instruction. Please read it if you haven't already. In it one will see that this righteous man lost everything he possessed, including his children. We learn about integrity when Job would not forsake God even though he felt he didn't deserve this catastrophe (Job 2: 9-10). We learn from Job about humility when Job was reminded, *"Where were you when I laid the foundations of the earth? Tell Me if you have understanding"* (Job 38:4). And near the end of this great story of "hanging in there," of Job's extraordinary perseverance through suffering, we learn how important it is to put others first because it was then the Lord double-blesses Job. He returns everything Job lost plus *"twice as much as he had before" "when he [Job] prayed for his friends"* (Job 42:10).

To bring this point on suffering closer to home, just before my visit with Julie and Keith, Xavier, who was about four years old at the time, pulled scalding hot water down on himself in an attempt to help his mother prepare a meal. It

was one of those times when you see a catastrophe about to happen, but you can't get there quickly enough. Julie just couldn't get to Xavier quickly enough. She rushed him to the hospital and found a burn specialist there, a miracle in itself when you consider the small town they live in. The treatment that was prescribed for Xavier involved bathing him every day to keep the burned area on his chest and chin clean and then applying ointment on the area to prevent infection.

Needless to say, this was all very painful for Xavier. And when I arrived shortly after his accident, I witnessed his screaming when he would yell at his parents, "Why are you doing this to me?" as Julie and Keith would take turns applying this very necessary treatment for him. It was painful to watch, and no amount of reassuring could comfort poor Xavier, who was in terrible pain. It was very difficult for Julie and Keith and me to watch also, as they had no desire to inflict this pain on their son. But they also knew if they didn't, Xavier could very well develop an infection and even die from his injury. Xavier recovered very quickly, with little noticeable scarring. Today, Xavier is a very sweet boy who loves the Lord and his parents deeply, knowing from experience that they care for him and his well-being very much. This was confirmed later when Xavier was six years old and approached his mother asking her about Jesus. After confirming that Xavier wanted to receive Jesus into his life, Julie led him in prayer that very same day.

One thing that I have learned for sure from my suffering is that there is a God who loves us very much, so much so that our Father in heaven sent His only Son to die for us and pay the price for our sin that we might live with Him for all eternity. And I believe with my whole heart that our Father doesn't like to watch us suffer any more than Julie and Keith wanted to see their son suffer or that He wanted to see Jesus suffer and die. But He also knows what is needed for our greater good, and as Jesus was raised from the dead, we will be, too, far above the pain and the suffering of this world. Jesus promises us that, *"God will wipe away every tear from their eyes; there shall be no more death, nor sorrow, nor crying. There shall be no more pain, for the former things have passed away"* (Revelation 21:4). And in Isaiah 25:8b–9, God promises, *"And the Lord GOD will wipe away tears from all faces; The rebuke of His people He will take away from all the earth; For the LORD has spoken. And it will be said in that day: 'Behold, this is our God; We have waited for Him, and He will save us. This is the LORD; We have waited for Him; We will be glad and rejoice in His salvation.'"*

Forgiveness

This "spirit of reconciliation" the Good Lord had given me, not only included the desire to reconcile relationships with there with me. The tears started to flow. I forgave them and asked for their forgiveness for all I had done against their wishes. We talked for I don't know how long and about other things as well. In looking back now it was like when we came together as a family many years before after my parents divorce and reconciliation. It was a wonderful time. Thank You, Lord Jesus!

Coming away from that experience was as if a heavy weight was being lifted off me, then God's peace filling me like never before. A few years after this wonderful experience I would receive confirmation of this reconciliation and an inspiration to write this book.

It happened when I visited my nephew Richard, who was named after my father, and he showed me a book my dad had written back in 1964, which I had never seen or even knew about before. The name of it is "Look to This Day" published by the Upper Room, but out of print today. It is a beautiful little book of inspirations and prayers for the handicapped, which my dad was also. After reading it I was comforted by it and I knew I wanted to write a follow on to his book. But it wasn't until I started this project, about two years after my visit with Rick, that I knew exactly what I was going to write. It is interesting to me also that the timing of receiving dad's book came after I was saved. Praise God for how He weaves the fabric of our lives.

As I have learned, we must give forgiveness before we can commune with God because in that way we have now shown to our Father in Heaven that we have forgiven as He has forgiven us. And as Jesus also said, *"leave your gift there before the altar, and go your way. First be reconciled to your brother, and then come and offer your gift"* (Matthew 5:24).

From my experience, I have also realized that forgiveness we give to others must also be given to ourselves. We must forgive ourselves. We are toughest on ourselves, more so sometimes, than anyone else. I know it was that way with me, especially because of my attempted suicide. After facing all the external conditions that contributed to my depression and subsequent suicide attempt, I was left with just myself. In helping me to deal with that the Lord taught me that if I was going to help others and *"love my neighbor as myself,"* then I had to have the love for myself He has for each one of us. Because how can I love my neighbor if I hate myself?

From what the Lord has taught me about loving oneself, I believe, is that loving oneself is not putting ourselves first, but rather putting others first and striving to see the love of Christ in them. Because what we see in others is a reflection of what we see in ourselves. *"To know the love of Christ which passes knowledge; that you may be filled with all the fullness of God"* (Ephesians 3:19).

Finally, I would like to leave you with these thoughts on suffering and forgiveness in our life. Jesus left us with seven key statements as He was dying on the cross that I hope will always shape my attitude and my character in any situation, but especially in time of suffering and forgiveness. He said:

1) "*Father, forgive them, for they do not know what they do*" (Luke 23:34). I must always forgive those who I believe have hurt me.
2) "*Assuredly, I say to you, today you will be with me in Paradise*" *(Luke 23:43).* After I seek forgiveness and ask Jesus into my life, I will see Jesus in Paradise someday. (see also Luke 11:4)

3) "*Woman, behold your son!...Behold your mother!*" (John 19:26-27). I should always consider others before myself.
4) "*My God, My God, why have you forsaken me?*" (Mark 15:34). It is all right to tell God my true feelings.
5) "*I thirst!*" (John 19:28). After others, I can certainly petition God for my needs and He wants me to.
6) "*It is finished!*" (John 19:30). My mission on earth is complete when God says it is complete.
7) "*Father, into Your hands I commit My spirit*" (Luke 23:46). In all things may God's will be the desire of my heart.

The key to the process of transformation—a continuing process until we are with the Lord—is to accept Jesus as Lord of our lives. And then ask for (Luke 11:13) and allow the Holy Spirit to work in our lives "*to will and to do according to His good pleasure*" (Philippians 2:13). Because God has given us a free will, He is looking for our agreement in making His will the "*desire of our heart.*" That is saying yes to God in everything. As I have found, without letting this supernatural Power act on our behalf, it is impossible for us to change and be separated from those things that are sinful and hurtful to God, our family, our friends, and others whom God puts in our lives. For Jesus said, "*But the Helper, the Holy Spirit, whom the Father will send in My name, He will teach you all things, and bring to your remembrance all things that I said to you*" (John 14:26). As we allow, this process will continue for the rest of our lives here on earth because, as Jesus says, "*I am the vine, you are the branches. He who abides in Me, and I in him, bears much fruit; for without Me you can do nothing*" (John 15:5). And as Paul went on to explain in his epistle, "*Being confident of this very thing, that He who has begun a good work in you will complete it until the day of Jesus Christ"* (Philippians 1:6). Praise God!!!

CHAPTER SIX

SHARING THE "GOOD NEWS"

Psalm 107:2
Let the redeemed of the LORD say so,
Whom He has redeemed from the hand of the enemy,

Romans 10:14
How then shall they call on Him in whom they have not believed? And how shall they believe in Him of whom they have not heard? And how shall they hear without a preacher?

1 Peter 3:15
But sanctify the Lord God in your hearts, and always be ready to give a defense to everyone who asks you a reason for the hope that is in you, with meekness and fear;

Psalm 34:1
I will bless the LORD at all times;
His praise shall continually be in my mouth.

After my first vision in the hospital and being told that I had to go back and fill in the empty box on the Tapestry of Hope, I came to believe that an important part of my mission would be to tell others of my experience. And the most important part of filling in that square was the realization of the saving grace of our God through our Lord Jesus Christ, which He wants to give to all who turn to Him. God is not a respecter of persons. He loves us all equally.

What I didn't know was how this "telling" would be accomplished. It wasn't until a year or so later when I was in the hospital again for more reconstruction surgery on my face that I had another vision. As before, I was before the tapestry. But this time, I was right in front of the empty square, and I was told to push on it. When I did, it fell inward like a panel, and out of it came a flood of writing right at me. Then the Lord's voice said, "Don't worry about what you will say. I will give you the words."

Since that time, it has never ceased to amaze me how He has used my experience since saving me to reach others and prevent them from going down the path I took. But more important, He has used it to draw others to know Him in a personal way through Jesus. However, I found out soon that my Lord would initiate these talks where, when, and to whom He wanted. I know this because anytime I tried to initiate a talk in front of a group on my own, it would not work out well at all. But on an individual basis, the Lord always gave me the words.

One of the first talks I gave was to a youth group, and after my testimony, two teenagers went to their parents and confessed that they were having the symptoms of depression that I described in my talk. One of the youths was hospitalized immediately.

As an aside, our Lord has many fine professionals whom He may work through for healing as He did with me. And even though I will be talking about some miraculous healings I witnessed, I do not want anyone to discount these normal channels for healing we have today. After all, Luke, the writer of the Gospel that bears his name was a physician. But God does work miraculously, I believe, when the natural way has reached its limit.

Another appointment to speak came one day when I received a call from someone who had heard about me and wondered if I would give my talk to a local high school. It seemed there had been two suicides within a six-month period, and they wanted me to talk at a general assembly for the school about my experience with depression and suicide. However, the principle got cold feet about the general assembly because I would talk about the Lord. How unfortunate and dangerous this whole issue of separation of church and state is. We are talking about potentially saving lives here, and they are worried I might talk about God. However, the Lord is in control, so some of the youth got permission to use a classroom before school, and we met there at 7 a.m.

The room was packed. Students were even out in the hall. Before I started my talk, I was asked if after my testimony I would invite anyone who wanted, to give his or her life to Jesus. I had never done this before, so I prayed that the Holy Spirit would give me the right words to say. As I was coming to a close in my talk, I sensed the voice of the Holy Spirit telling what to do. He had me invite those who wanted to commit their lives to Christ and also those who wanted to recommit their lives to Jesus to raise their hands as a sign of that commitment. This way, they wouldn't feel intimidated or embarrassed, since no one would be singled out as a non-believer. Well, when I gave that invitation, every hand in the place went up. I didn't see anyone whose hand was not up. It was amazing, simply amazing! God's amazing grace at work!

Going Deeper

Though the Lord was using me to reach others through the testimony He had given me, I still had (and still have) a lot to learn about Him. However, He soon revealed to me that even more important than knowing about Him was coming to know Him in a deeper way. This deeper revelation came to me while I was traveling to see my daughter Sue and her family in Oregon. It would instill in me the "fear of God," the reverence and honor that is due our Sovereign and Almighty God. It came in a way that I will never forget and that will always remind me, I pray, never to take my God for granted.

On the way to Oregon, I picked up my sister, Laurie, in Denver, and we traveled together to Jackson Hole, Wyoming, to do some camping. Laurie instilled the love of hiking in me there, and we proceeded to hike halfway around Lake Genny and up into the mountains a little way. It was a time of reconnecting with Laurie after many years of being away in my own world fulfilling selfish desires. It was a wonderful time together and a blessing!

After a few days of enjoying this most beautiful part of the world, Laurie returned to her home in Colorado while I continued on to see Sue and her family. But first I wanted to finish the hike around the lake that Laurie and I had started.

If you have ever been to Jackson, Wyoming, you will understand that words are not enough to describe the beauty and strength of the mountains there. I believe the power and majesty of God are visible in those mountains,. It is beyond me that anyone can look at this wonderful world that God created for us and not believe in Him. What a tragedy not to enjoy Him and His creation for us.

The day started out bright and sunny. The first part of my hike was at the base of the mountains; then as I came to the side of the lake that Laurie and I had not completed, I found myself looking right into those mountains. It was a magnificent sight. I remember looking at the two mountains in front of me with a valley between them and being almost frozen in my tracks by the beauty of this sight.

The sky was completely overcast now. It was a solid overcast. There were no individual clouds, just a gray sky overhead. Then I saw it. It was a puff of a cloud that appeared between the two majestic mountains, ascended to the mountain peak to my left, and encircled its peak. I thought, this must be something like what the children of Israel witnessed when they came to the Mountain of God in the desert before receiving the Ten Commandments from God.

Then this puff of a cloud descended the mountain, came to the center of the lake, and hovered directly in front of me. It was then that I realized that something special was taking place. When this cloud was encircling the mountain peak, I wondered if it could be an angel. Now I was sure it was because he seemed to be looking directly at me as he hovered over the lake. I don't know what possessed me, but I took a picture of him, but then he retreated to the far side of the lake. This sudden departure by the angel made me feel irreverent in taking a picture at the special moment of our meeting.

Next, the small cloud linked up with and started to follow a much larger cloud. Immediately I knew I was in the presence of God and dropped to my knees. Then the battle started in my mind. "You're kneeling on this path. What if someone comes along and finds you like this." I listened to that voice, so I stood up. Then the power of God overwhelmed me, and I remember thinking, I am in the presence of God, and I am worried about what someone else thinks! I dropped to my knees and stayed there. During that time, I had the sense of what an insignificant speck of dust I was in the presence of God Almighty. I could now understand how the children of Israel felt when they said to Moses, "You speak with us, and we will hear; but let not God speak with us, lest we die" (Exodus 20:19). I hate to admit this, but I wanted to leave this place as soon as I could. I felt so unworthy and afraid to be in His Holy Presence.

But it was as if I was nailed to that spot. I couldn't get up and run away as I wanted to. Then the angel escorted the Lord from my sight but returned in that puff of a cloud that seemed to cover him. He hovered over the lake one last time until, all of a sudden, he seemed to send something like two silver arrows in my direction. Then he disappeared.

As I got off my knees, two hikers came down the path from the opposite direction I had been traveling and went by me. It was if time had restarted after standing still while I was in the presence of our King. All I could do was just about run from that spot while looking over my shoulder as I went down the path.

Whatever I had envisioned God to be before, I now knew He was beyond what I could ever imagine and that He required of me all the reverence, respect, and honor that is due Him. It was time to come to know Him, not just to know about Him. In looking back now on this epiphany in my life, it was time to fix my eyes on Jesus, the personification of God, if I was ever going to know God in a personal and loving way.

Fortunately, when we accept Jesus into our lives, He gives us His Holy Spirit to work in us those changes needed for us to come into that deeper relationship with God. He provides the righteousness that covers us, which is needed so when we stand in our Father's presence, He sees Jesus, not our *"filthy rags."*

Reaching Others

The Holy Spirit also works through us to reach others for Christ, sometimes in spite of ourselves. This became evident when I visited a long-time friend who did not know Jesus in a personal way. Bette Jo was into a lot of "new age" beliefs, so it should not have been a surprise to me that the Lord wanted to reach her. When we met in 1999, I had this tremendous urge to tell her about Jesus, but I felt inadequate in doing so. I was all hung up in what would be the right things to say. Would I remember the right Scripture to quote? and on and on. If only I had remembered what the Lord had told me earlier about how He would provide the words.

It was a frustrating time to say the least. At one point I blurted out, "Well, if you had the cure for cancer, wouldn't you want to tell others about it?" I could see I was getting nowhere, and if anything, I was just driving her farther away from her Savior. Finally, she had had enough and we parted, not even saying good-bye to each other. This mission was a total failure, and as I traveled down the highway, I told God I was sorry for being such a failure and wondered why He had even allowed me to talk to Bette Jo at all.

During Christmas time that year, which was a few months after my visit to see Bette Jo, I received this beautiful Christmas card from her and it had a verse from the Gospel of Luke about our Savior on it. It really surprised me, especially because she was not a believer but she sent this beautiful card anyway. I called her to thank her for being so thoughtful, and after we exchanged pleasantries, she proceeded to tell me about the incredible experience she had.

She said, "You know, after you left, I received 'The Jesus Film' in the mail." If you are not familiar with this movie on audiocassette, it is about who Jesus is and why we need Him as our Savior. Its powerful message from the Book of Luke, which has been translated into many languages, has been used by our Lord to bring thousands to Christ around the world. I should have realized what was coming next from Bette Jo, but I am ashamed to say I was expecting the worst. She continued, "Well, I looked at that tape, and at the end they give the sinner's prayer. And you know what?" I was hanging on every word now. "I said it."

All I could say at this point was, Praise God!!! No other words came into my mind but "Praise God!" I just kept saying, "Praise God!" It was truly the work of the Holy Spirit, not me. Then she said, "You know, if you had not talked to me that day, I would never have looked at that tape." It was from this experience that I learned that the Holy Spirit will work through us in spite of ourselves. He just wants a willing spirit to work with. Later I learned that "The Jesus Film" had arrived--the very day we parted!

Bette Jo continues to grow in the Lord, and recently she told me she met the pastor who was responsible for sending out "The Jesus Film" at that perfect time for her to receive it. What a blessing that must have been. And I thank that pastor for his obedience to our Lord in taking that brave step to send out the Lord's tape to many in the area, in pure faith that it would reach others for Him. Praise God!!!

Prayer

Another lesson God taught me about His power had to do with prayer for others. Once when I was working as a part-time bus driver for a well-known theme park, I was taking a busload of guests back to their resort. All the seats were filled, and there was hardly any standing room. Way back in the bus, I could hear an infant screaming. It was that type of cry that tells you something is wrong versus the child being tired or just wanting attention. It was a desperate and pathetic cry. I started to pray for this baby that the Lord would provide his or her needs because I had no idea what the problem was. Shortly, the crying stopped, and a peace, His Peace, took over the bus. As the guests departed the bus, a woman carrying a baby on her shoulder came by me, and as she stepped down the stairs, her baby was looking directly at me with big wide-open eyes. I knew it was the baby I had prayed for, and as this baby looked right into my eyes, I felt Jesus coming through this little child of God. What an awesome and personal God we serve.

At another time, I was asked to take a family back to their hotel because their child was sick. It was one of those rare times when there was no one else on the bus. Before we left, I felt led to ask them if I could pray for their child. They agreed and so I did. When they got off the bus, they thanked me for praying for their child because she was already feeling better. Again the Lord was using a circumstance in a person's life, in this case a whole family's, to reveal Himself to others in a special way. It also encourages us when we see how our God hears and answers prayer.

Sharing My Testimony

It would be hard to think of one time of giving the testimony the Lord has given me that would be more special than another. Certainly those times when the Lord revealed to me how He was using the testimony are special. After almost every talk, people come up to me and thank me for sharing, and that is always encouraging. But when I hear and or see the impact of it on someone else's life, it is always humbling and reinforces what I have learned—it is all about Jesus, not about me. We are not defined by our experiences but by our relationship with God.

Sharing my testimony with the young people is always a blessing to me. It is always exciting to be asked to tell a youth group about trusting in the Lord and how we can always depend on Him. I know that if the Lord reaches young men and women now, what a rewarding life they would have ahead of them. Not that they will have an easy time of it by any stretch of the imagination, but when they depend on Jesus, He will get them through everything as He did–and continues to do–for me. *"I can do all things through Christ who strengthens me"* (Philippians 4:13).

I love to work and will work with any Christian, Jewish, or other organization that will have me. This is why it has been so rewarding for me, for example, to work with the youth group at St. Paul's Presbyterian Church near Orlando when I am in Florida. They are a wonderful group led by "Scooby" Phelps and pastored by Bryan Stamper. Also, my friends there continue to keep in touch with me by e-mail and lift me up in prayer while I am on the road, which is so encouraging. When He leads it is always exciting to see how the Lord will work in the lives He brings across our path.

Not too long ago, our Lord brought a young man into my life through my testimony given at the Narkis Street Congregation in Jerusalem. Benjamin (not his real name) was having a very difficult time dealing with the suicide of his former girlfriend, and as he told me, he felt compelled, though he didn't know why, to come to church that day. We talked and met a few times over a couple of weeks after that, and when I last saw him, he was smiling and happy again and enjoying his friends with him. I could see he was a new person. God had used His saving experience with me to help this previously very sad and depressed young man.

One might ask, "How do you know the Lord orchestrated this whole event?" Well, on the day I gave the talk that Benjamin heard, I had no idea I was even going to give my testimony. The pastor of the Narkis Street Congregation, Charles Koop, all of a sudden interrupted his service and called me up to the platform to give my testimony. That is the power of God's love for us. He will meet us right where we are at, regardless. Halleluyah!!!

There is an aspect of my testimony that I have to be sensitive about and aware of as I relate the Lord's story of my redemption: there is almost always someone in the audience who is suffering depression, may have attempted suicide, or had a loved one or a friend who committed suicide. It is a sensitive situation because here I am cured and alive but they or someone they know are not. In every case where that was an issue the Lord has made it known to me and He handled it beautifully.

For example, when I was volunteering at the Bible College of Wales in the summer of 2003, I was asked to give my testimony just before I left the college. It was at their Sunday service, and they were getting ready to receive their students from around the world for a new term. Among the group that day in church was a couple from South Africa who had just arrived to work at the college. This day, and it had happened before, the Lord prompted me to say the following during my talk.

"Just because I am here and someone you may know who is not here because of a suicide it does not mean that person is not with the Lord." Certainly, I can testify to the truth that God is in control of every situation because I know what can happen in those split seconds before death as was in my case when I called upon the Lord in my desperation. Also, I know I am only back among the living because of the will of God and that He still had a purpose for me to fulfill here on earth.

After my testimony, the couple from South Africa came up to me, elated and full of joy, to thank me. My look must have telegraphed my wonder about why the wife was thanking me, so she then proceeded to tell me the reason for their joy. She said that during my talk, the Lord had given her peace about her mother, who had committed suicide. I cannot express the appropriate words of thanks and praise to our Almighty God when His love and compassion for us comes through in such a dramatic way as at this moment. I am always at a loss for words at times like this and just say a simple, Praise God!!! I know it was the Lord's words and not mine that comforted this couple. But I believe when our will is linked to God's will, His full Redemptive Power is brought to bear on any situation He has placed us in (Matthew 7:8).

The 9th Wave

Once released, God's Redemptive Power continues causing a ripple effect like a giant wave rolling through whatever is in its path. For example, have you ever been at the seashore just watching the waves, and every so often, a larger wave comes crashing in? There doesn't seem to be any reason this happens. No storm is blowing in nor are there any other changes in the weather that we can see that might cause the swells to change. I was reading somewhere that this phenomenon is called "the 9th Wave." And supposedly one can count the waves after one large one and the next large wave will be the ninth. I have never tested this principle at a beach, but the next time I am at the seashore I will!

However, the way the Lord works in our lives to affect others is like the 9th Wave sometimes. We don't actually see the Lord working in our lives or the lives of our families, friends, and others around us, but we know He is. Then all of a sudden, the Lord brings the 9th Wave into our lives, and we can't help but notice what He did. And all we can do is thank God and praise Him.

The Lord's Power was manifested in this way after my testimony in a little town in Israel, called Qatrine, very near the Syrian border. A very depressed man came to Pastor Ronnen's worship service. The pastor ministers there and in the Tiberius area of Galilee. Boris (not his real name) had become very depressed and could focus only on the things that were going wrong in his life. He admitted to being dependent on alcohol. Boris was a new believer, and the enemy was doing everything he could to convince Boris he was not saved. As we prayed for Boris after service that day, we could see his countenance change almost immediately. The Lord was pouring His healing mercies upon Boris as we were praying, right before our eyes. It was wonderful to behold!.

As God's wave of grace poured out, not only did those changes continue for Boris but they were manifested by his deliverance from depression and dependency on alcohol.

His mother saw these changes when he visited her and soon answered Pastor Ora's alter call at Praise Chapel-Israel and received Jesus into her life. Again God used what He had done for others, in this case a son, to change a heart and brought this mother into a saving relationship with Him through Jesus.

When their jailer asked Paul and Silas what he must do to be saved, they replied, *"Believe on the Lord Jesus Christ, and you will be saved,* ***you and your household****"* (Acts 16:31, emphasis added). We could certainly see Boris's household coming into our Lord's Kingdom as God's giant 9th wave of grace.

Another example of how the Lord fulfills His promise to also save one's household happened within my own family. This was also another opportunity by the Lord for me to seek forgiveness for a broken relationship that I caused.

A few years ago when I was living in Florida my second wife, Jeanne and mother of our beautiful daughter Stephanie, asked if I would give the Lord's testimony in my life to her church. This came right out of the blue because we had only talked a few times before that, but it was typical as most of these opportunities have happened like this before. But we know Who is in charge of these circumstances, thank God.

Of course I accepted and came to her lovely church and was warmly received by Pastor Scott and his congregation. Before my talk the pastor asked if I would give my testimony at all his services, to which I gladly agreed. But then in the second service the Pastor Scott did something I had not expected. He told his congregates that he was foregoing his sermon to give me that time to talk about my experience in coming to the Lord. What an unselfish act by Pastor Scott and it gave glory to God for His mercy for yet another soul that has that privilege to share with others.

During one service I publicly asked for Jeanne's forgiveness. Thank God He gives us the "spirit of reconciliation." I could not have done this or been here to do what was right without the Lord's love, grace and mercy.

Sometime afterward Jeanne told me that she had come to accept Jesus into her life because of what I had gone through. As Jeanne said, "I didn't want to wait till I reached the point you did before receiving the Lord into my life!" Oh, how our Lord can turn what seems hopeless in our lives to His Goodness for others and us! (Romans 8:28). Praise God!!!

Another Kind of Deliverance

There is a kind of deliverance the Lord works through us that is not taken very seriously. In fact, I cannot remember when I last heard a sermon about it. But in the Gospels it is mentioned some fifty-six times. This deliverance is from the demonic presence and evil among us.

Believe me, demonic presence is something I do not look for or want to come up against. But I do desire discernment about it so that when I am facing this evil, I know I'll have the Lord's power to deal with it and I will not fear it (Psalm 23:4). The Lord does give us protection against these *"principalities and powers"* with His *"armor of God"* described in Ephesians 6:10–18. This armor includes prayer, and I pray, "Lord please keep me from evil that I may not cause pain" (1 Chronicles 4:10).

When I first came up against this presence, I was not ready for it, nor did I see it for what it was until the Lord finally revealed it to me; and then He dealt with it. In looking back on that experience, I can see God was answering my prayer for discernment.

It happened in Oxford, England. I had been asked by a new friend, Franz, to come to his house and give my testimony to some friends he had invited for the evening. After we met each other and socialized a little, Franz asked if he could tape my talk so he could send it to other friends. I agreed, got set up, and began to share my experience of God's grace and mercy. Soon a young woman, whom I'll call Diane, came in and sat down. She was suffering with severe depression. As I continued to talk, I suddenly felt a weight on me, and I could not concentrate. I stumbled for words because they were not pouring forth as they usually did. However, I discounted the whole thing as the result of being distracted.

At church the following Sunday when Franz and I ran into Diane again, I felt that same weight and the inability to concentrate. I realized this was not just an aberration. It was then that I knew I was dealing with something coming from this young woman. I asked her if I could pray for her, and she agreed. As I prayed, I found it hard again to find the words and noticed that her countenance would change from a smile to utter gloom. I had also witnessed this at Franz's house. After I prayed and she left, there was a feeling of incompleteness. I did not feel released from the situation, but I did not know what to do.

After the service, Franz and I walked to the front of the church because he wanted to introduce me to his friend who gave the sermon. As Franz was talking to another friend, I noticed the young woman again. It was then that the Lord put on my heart—so strongly that I knew it was from Him—to deliver this woman from the spirit that possessed her. It was a struggle for me because many people were still milling about, and I wondered, Should I do this now? But when the Lord puts something that strongly on your heart, you know you must obey, so I walked over to her and asked if she would like to be delivered. I could see the struggle going on within her, but finally an almost pitiful cry came out. "Yes," she answered, so the Lord delivered her right then and there. It was awesome for me to witness that Redemptive Power of our Lord, and I was glad that I had obeyed Him.

As Franz and I were leaving the church, Diane came over to us, and we could see the change the Lord had made in her. Her whole disposition had changed. She simply beamed, and now a new Spirit was living within her, His Holy Spirit. Diane is a dear sister in the Lord now because of her conscious decision, which the Lord honored. Praise God!!!

Needless to say, this experience taught me that demonic presence in our world is very real and must be combated at every turn. But I must stress that we cannot combat this evil with our own strength or intelligence. No one by himself or herself will outsmart the devil. This evil one has been dealing with the weaknesses of human beings far too long to be outsmarted by our own flesh. That is why it is imperative, and I say again, it is imperative not to venture into his territory. Anytime we put anything between God and us, we are venturing into the enemy's territory. But Jesus gives us His power over the enemy (Luke 10:19), and we need not fear the devil. However, we must keep praying, as in the Lord's Prayer, *"Lead us not into temptation but deliver us from the evil one."* By our good choices and conscious decisions, our Lord God will lead us in His paths of righteousness. In fact, if we have integrity of heart God will keep us from sinning against Him (Genesis 20:6).

Thus far, the Lord has taken me across the United States and to Haiti, the UK and Israel to work and to share His amazing love in my life, which He offers to everyone. These have been His opportunities "*for His good purpose.*"

Your Testimony

I am not unique by any stretch of the imagination. All believers have special and powerful stories about how the Lord came into their lives and what He is doing in their lives now. And these testimonies should be shared every time the Lord gives us opportunities (*"Let the redeemed of the Lord say so"*), whether it is in front of a group or individually with people He will bring across our paths. As a young believer, Ashley, shared with me recently, "Our testimonies are the Fifth Gospel." After all, the Gospels of Matthew, Mark, Luke, and John in the Bible are personal testimonies of their life with Christ. Therefore, like the Apostles, the Lord will put us in environments where He will enable us to speak or demonstrate "our" Gospel for His glory and praise. And again, there is no need to worry about what we are to say or do, because, rest assured, the Holy Spirit will lead us in helping others according to what He has already done in our lives.

Please do not keep what the Lord has done for you to yourself. It just may be what someone else needs to hear and see in order to cope and survive in this world and be equipped to enter eternity. If we had the cure for cancer, wouldn't we share it? Well, when we have Jesus as our Lord and Savior, we have His gift of Salvation so that we can live with Him forever. Please share His gift with others!

"For we are to God the fragrance of Christ among those who are being saved and among those who are perishing" (2 Corinthians 2:15).

Halleluyah!!!

CHAPTER SEVEN

JESUS RANSOMED (AND REDEEMED) YOU AND ME

Mark 10:45
"For even the Son of Man did not come to be served, but to serve, and to give His life a ransom for many."

Psalm 111:9
He has sent redemption to His people;
He has commanded His covenant forever:
Holy and awesome is His name.

John 14:6
Jesus said to him, "I am the way, the truth, and the life. No one comes to the Father except through Me."

Here we are, some 2000 years since Jesus was here on earth, and even history attests to the truth of His words. Reynolds Price, writing about "Jesus of Nazareth" in the December 1999 issue of "Time" magazine, said, "A serious argument can be made that no one else's life has proved as powerful and enduring as that of Jesus."

However, the question continues to be asked, Who is Jesus? Jesus is the personification of God, who meets us where we are so that He can bring us into a right relationship with Him. From my experience, I know how true those words are. As He met the Samaritan woman at the well, He met me at the bottom of the well of despair. That, I would hope, is a place no one will have to be to meet Jesus. It is one reason for this book. But the most important point is that Jesus is knocking right now at the door of the hearts of those who do not know Him, wanting to come into their lives and establish a personal relationship with God.

For some, that relationship is established instantaneously, but for me it has been more a process of coming to know and trust my Lord God. He knows us better than we know ourselves, so He knows how to develop that personal bond with us. He led me in baby steps first and then in very powerful ways to develop that personal relationship between us. And He continues to develop it.

One day after I had been released from the hospital for the first time, my wife Ginny and I were at home, and she asked me if I would be all right for a few minutes while she went to the store. She was a little hesitant about leaving me alone, but the store was very close to where we lived. I said I would be OK, so she left. Almost immediately I could feel myself sinking into a depressive state. My support was gone, and there was no one there to talk to. I started to pray, "Please God, do not let me sink into that pit again."

Immediately the phone rang. On the other end was a man named Larry Girtin. I had never met him; however, he was from the Rotary club I had belonged to, and later we became very good friends. He said, "I heard about you, and I was wondering if when you felt better, I could take you out to lunch at one of the next Rotary meetings." Almost immediately I could feel my spirit being uplifted. It was as if God was on the other end of the line. We talked some more and made a tentative date; then just as I was hanging up, Ginny walked back into the room. She saw that I had been on the phone and asked, "Who was that on the phone?" I replied, "God."

That experience was another epiphany for me. Although there were many ups and downs ahead, it was God's way of showing me He is real and He wants to help me. He wants me to come to know Him, trust Him more and to depend on Him. As an aside, later I felt compelled to get a license plate with the letters "TRSTNHM." I knew that God wanted me always to remember to "Trust in Him."

The next major encouragement and guidance from the Lord came about six months later, after the second surgery to rebuild my face. This encounter was when God instilled in me the desire to read and study His Word, the Bible. And it was this nudge into His Word that led me to knowing God in a deeper, more personal way through Jesus Christ. "The way" (our path to God), "the truth" (God of the Bible manifested for us in the flesh), "and the life" We are a new creation—ransomed, forgiven, and washed clean by God's sacrifice for us through the blood of His Son Jesus (John 14:6; 2 Corinthians 5:17; Mark 10:45; 1 Corinthians 6:11).

Ginny and I had gone to Baltimore, where two of the most caring, dedicated and proficient surgeons I have ever known started their two years of work on me. Drs. Paul Manson and Norman Clark worked as a team at Johns Hopkins Hospital and performed a very difficult but, as it turned out, very successful surgery in the initial rebuilding of my decimated face. This particular surgery was some eighteen hours long.

Without going into too much detail (which I couldn't anyway), the good doctors removed the fibula from my left leg to reconstruct my jaw, then removed some two to three ribs to rebuild my face, since most, if not all, of my face bones were shattered by the suicide bullet. It would be two weeks before I recovered enough to be able to leave the hospital.

Ginny's cousin Nancy and her family had a house on the outskirts of Baltimore and invited us to stay there overnight before we caught the train to Stamford and Ginny's mom where we would recoup and I would heal from surgery before making the long trip back to Kansas. We were both hitting bottom mentally, physically, and spiritually from these circumstances related to my attempt at suicide and now the recovery process. Ginny was exhausted, and I was reeling from my surgeries. My head was as big as a watermelon, and I was on crutches because of the surgery on my leg to remove the fibula. It just seemed so overwhelming to us.

Nancy had told Ginny to make sure she allowed plenty of time for the cab to take us to the train station because it would come from the city. And when you called for a taxi, you could never predict when it would arrive. However, when Ginny called for the cab, it seemed that it was there in no time. After the driver helped us with our bags and into the cab, he got into the taxi and never looked back at us. But as he was driving, he began to minister to us in a powerful and uplifting way. This angel—I believe he was an angel and I think Ginny does, too—was sent from God to bring us His comfort and to lead us to know Him through Jesus. His words as he started to minister to us will forever be in my heart. He said, "God knows you are hurting, and He wants you to step back and take this time to learn about Him."

This cab driver continued to minister to us until we arrived at the train station. I can tell you it seemed as though we floated out of that taxi and onto our train. We joked later that we should have asked him to drive us all the way to Stamford instead of taking the train. That is how uplifting and inspiring his words were to us. I will never forget that encounter with one of God's ministering angels.

From that experience came an intense desire to read and study God's Word. As soon as we returned to our home in Kansas, I started inquiring about Bibles. I had no idea what I should be looking for, let alone studying. That is when Millie Stamm one of the saints our Lord surrounded us with, came to my rescue and provided me with the NIV Study Bible. Millie proved to be a dear friend and sister in Jesus until she passed away into our Lord's presence just a few years later. Then another new friend in the Lord, Frances Weisbein, brought me another Bible. And even my first wife, Faye, who continued to pray for our children and my salvation after we were divorced, sent me a Bible. Soon I had more Bibles than I knew what to do with!

Not having any discernment about these things I started to read the Bible like a novel. I started on page 1, Genesis, chapter 1, verse 1, and began to read. Almost from the beginning, I could sense Jesus in these words and accepted Him into my life. It is hard to explain, but there He was leading me in learning about Him, the God of my salvation. I found an outline in the Study Bible of the prophecies about Jesus, and immediately compiled a little book titled "Messianic Prophecies." I couldn't wait to share it with Ginny and others. I remember handing a copy to Ginny as if to say, Read this and you will know why Jesus is the Messiah. It was done out of arrogant self-righteousness and got the response it deserved. Oh, did I have a lot to learn—and still do! It was as if I had discovered something that nobody else knew, and I remember sending my findings to other ministries for their use. Needless to say, I never heard from any of the recipients, because as I was to learn later, it is Jesus and not me who does the saving. And it is our Father in heaven who gives us to Jesus (John 6:37; 17:9), as He did for me, by the power of His Holy Spirit. In this way, we come to know about God and develop a personal relationship with Him through Jesus because Jesus personifies God in a way we, as finite human beings, can understand and can relate to.

My study of the Bible continued in this way for the next couple of years. During that time I read through the Bible more than twice. In fact, the first time I read through the Bible under no set schedule, I finished the Old Testament on Christmas Eve and started the New Testament on Christmas Day, reading about Christ's birth. Our God is a God of order.

After reading the Bible through two-plus times, I knew there was more within His words, but it was not coming through to me. I remember asking God about this. Shortly after that prayer, the phone rang. And guess who it was? Yes, it was Larry Girtin calling to ask me if I would like to go to a Bible study with him. Knowing this was from the Lord, I agreed, and for about five years, Larry and I went every Monday night to Bible Study Fellowship (BSF), a non-denominational Bible study group that I highly recommend to any who want to further their study of God's Word. It is a very effective study of the Bible because it stresses letting the Bible interpret itself through the Holy Spirit rather then depending on commentaries by others.

God is talking to us through His Word that we might learn from Him about Him and His plan for the redemption for all mankind and specifically His plan for our lives. It is not that we learn God's word but that we let Him **reveal** what He is saying to us through it and we can not do that unless we are in His Bible. However, this is not to say we cannot gain insight from other personal commentaries and testimonies, but always check these against God's Bible to see if you receive confirmation in your spirit from Him directly. This of course includes even my own testimony you are reading now.

During our fifth year of study together, Larry passed from this life to be with our Lord forever. Larry was a beautiful friend and brother in the Lord, and I miss him and his wise counsel. However, I am happy for Larry to be where he is in that "cloud of witnesses" talked about in Hebrews 12:1. I am sure when Larry met Jesus, he heard Him say, *"Well done good, and faithful servant."*

My study of Scripture continued for the next two years in the BSF program, completing all the modules they provided for study at that time. During those seven years of study with BSF, I also studied two years of Judaism with the Florence Melton Program. This study was invaluable to me because it gave me a greater understanding of the people and the culture Jesus was born into as man, and, more important, as Teacher and Messiah. He brought the message of repentance and salvation to the Jew *first* and then to the Gentile (non-Jew) (Romans 1:16).

The Only Way

Why is accepting Jesus and the resulting obedience to God the only way we can be with Him for all eternity? It is really very simple. If God had not provided the way for our salvation, we could devise any plan that suited our fancy, one devoid of any laws or precepts, to get into heaven. However, just as is shown time and again in the Bible, *faith* in Jesus will always provide the way to our Father and Creator. Jesus said, *"I am the way, the truth, and the life. No one comes to the Father except through Me"* (John 14:6).

But why must we be saved? Because, on our own, we are incapable of living a life that is righteous enough to earn us a place in heaven to live forever with our Holy God. Let's face it. All we have to do is look at the situation of our world today, with hatred and violence becoming so prevalent that we are de-sensitized to its effects on our lives and our children's lives. If we would cancel our cable TV subscriptions and not support companies that sponsor the filth that comes into our living rooms today, for example, the entertainment industry would change overnight. But we can't (or won't) even do that.

In the United States alone, there are more than 33,000,000 laws, whereas God gave us the Ten which were inscribed on stone so that at that time, I believe, they could not be erased from our hearts of stone. Plus He gave us 603 other laws that covered, as a few examples, how to take care of our land, how to treat employees, and what is healthy for us to eat. But instead of abiding by those laws, we came up with our own. Now we have no concern for the sanctity of life, let alone loving our neighbor. Our lands are so polluted with insecticides that we are poisoning ourselves every day. Have you looked at the warning label on toothpaste lately? If you haven't and you have a child under six in the house, lock your toothpaste in the medicine cabinet.

It is so important, as I have learned to daily read the Bible. I start each day and end each day reading God's Word. It is one of the ways He communicates with us, and it is His guide to life and for life. As gifted apologist David Pawson said, it is "a love story about a Father who is in search of a bride for His Son."

The Bible begins in Genesis with the institution of marriage (Genesis 2:24) soon after God created Adam and Eve. He then married the Israelites, after delivering them from bondage in Egypt, at the Mountain of God and provided them the marriage covenant (Katuba), the Ten Commandments. Later God's Son, our Messiah, is born in Bethlehem of Judea to be *"the way, the truth, and the life"* for reconciliation to our Father in Heaven as His bride for all eternity. I believe this is why the Bible ends, in the Book of Revelation, with the wedding of Jesus and all His believers as His bride, reconciled to our Father in Heaven for all eternity.

Why is the Bible so important for our lives here on earth? God gave us the Bible so we would have His guidebook, not man's. It is His plan for us to be reconciled with Him forever and to *'love our neighbors as ourselves."* Unfortunately, there are people who have devised their own plan, (and their own gods) from their own sources and try to convince others that their way is the correct one. Just look in any self-help section of a bookstore, and you will see many books on "the" way to your own spirituality, to get rich, get a job, find the perfect mate, be successful, and on and on. This is why I like to tell others to read the Bible for themselves. Let God talk to you directly and show you His plan for your life (Jeremiah 29:11).

With that being said, let me try to convey what God's plan of redemption is and how we become the bride for His Son. We must remember we were all created with a free will and in God's image—body, soul, and spirit. Our first parents, Adam and Eve, after being tempted in the Garden of Eden decided to do it their way and disobeyed God, knowing the punishment was death. Why was the punishment death? Because sin separates us from God who is holy, *"but of the tree of the knowledge of good and evil you shall not eat, for in the day that you eat of it you shall surely die,"* (Genesis 2:17). Therefore, all humankind inherited their sin condition. An analogy to the inheritance of this sin condition might be like when we see children of alcoholic parents become alcoholics themselves. However, in God's love and mercy for us, He came down to this earth in the form of His Son, Jesus, to pay the penalty—death—for us so that we would not be eternally separated from God.

It is much like this analogy from a famous preacher: If we were to commit a crime, we would stand before a judge, and expect the judge to pronounce sentence on us. However, all of a sudden, the judge gets off his bench, comes down by our side, and offers to pay the judgment for us. We can believe the judge and accept his offer, or we can decide to let the judgment stand. It is our choice. Jesus said, *"I am the way, the truth, and the life. No one comes to the Father except through Me"* (John 14:6).

The two visions that I described in Chapter Four dealt with what it would be like without God. One of them was so horrible, as I mentioned, that the closest description I can give is knowing you're having a nightmare but you can't wake up.

In the vision of the Tapestry of Hope, described in Chapter Three, there were squares filled in with writing that described all the good things I had done in my life. But there was one square in which there was no writing; it was blank and I had to go back and fill it in. For a long time I thought there was just something I had to do. But God showed me that there was nothing I could do to earn heaven and a life with Him. If it were the good works that I had done in my life, I would be in heaven with Him now. He showed me that all I had to do was to accept His forgiveness of my sins. He paid the price for them through Jesus, God in the flesh, sacrificing His life and paying the penalty for my sins by shedding His blood for me. The Bible tells us, *"For it is the blood that makes atonement for the soul"* (Leviticus 17:11; Hebrews 9:22).

I have reflected on that, and I know there is no way I could stand before Almighty God and say, "I deserve to be in heaven with You because I have done these good things." What arrogance it would be on my part to think I knew what God wanted of me without letting Him show me. Any parent knows that for children to learn what is expected of them, they have to be shown. I love my Lord God and am thankful for the mercy and love He gave to me through Jesus. I also know that I am alive today to share what He has shown me with everyone He gives me the chance to, which, I believe, is part of filling in that empty square in the tapestry.

When we receive Jesus into our lives, we start to understand, know, and establish the personal and intimate relationship with God that He wants with all of us. It isn't a religion; it is a relationship. As I mentioned earlier, right after God created Adam and Eve he created the institution of marriage (Genesis 2:24), that close, intimate, and personal relationship between a man and a woman. And when one thinks about a family relationship within this institution you can see what holds this it all together is obedience (childlike), faithfulness (spouse) and love (father). I believe God did this to show us the kind of relationship He wants to have with all of us—forever.

Since I accepted Jesus, God, into my life, I have been blessed in so many ways. Not that my life has been a bed of roses, which it hasn't, but blessed because I know He is always with me through thick and thin. He has given me the "ministry of reconciliation" (2 Corinthians 5:18), which has helped me immensely in seeking forgiveness and reconciliation with my family and others whom I have wronged.

This is an ongoing process. It is a difficult one for me because of the pride that has been in me, which needs to be fully replaced by God's humility, the humility God displayed for us by coming off His throne and leaving His glory in heaven, becoming a man and paying our penalty—death—so that we all could be saved and live. May we never forget what it cost God to do that selfless act for us.

In Chapter Five, I went into some examples of the transformation that I experienced. Suffice it to say that I find myself losing the desire to do things that hurt God, others, and myself because God is by His Holy Spirit working in me *"to will and to do according to His good pleasure"* (Philippians 2:13). It is not that I don't fail or miss the mark today, because I do, but when I do, the Lord's grace picks me up, I confess my wrong to God, ask for the help I need not to do it anymore (repent), and move on. My words do not do justice in describing how much God loves you and me and how He wants none to perish (to die and be without Him) but all to come to repentance and receive His gift of Salvation through Jesus.

I know my words alone cannot convince anyone of the saving relationship God wants to have with us, but Jesus can. All I suggest is you ask God yourself to show you the truth, because it will "set you free" (John 8:32) and He will show you (Matthew 7:7). Also by reading the Bible God will talk to you directly as He does to me. Please let God reveal Himself to you and the plan He has for you *"to give you hope and a future;"* His path to Him through Jesus for a blessed life here on earth and the life to come with Him for all eternity. Doesn't it make more sense to enjoy the treasures God has for us now than to try one's own way, like I did; and find out the hard way one cannot live a righteous life without God?

Oswald Chambers in his wonderful devotional "My Utmost for His Highest" provides a great summary for us. He said, "Until we know Jesus, God is a mere abstraction, we cannot have faith in Him; but immediately we hear Jesus say, *'He that hath seen Me hath seen the Father,'* we have something real, and faith is boundless. Faith is the whole man rightly related to God by the power of the Spirit of Jesus Christ." (Devotion for Oct. 30th)

And, as if to add an exclamation point to this and by a set of circumstances that only the Lord could orchestrate to lead me here, I am in Israel writing this chapter. Not only am I in Israel, but I am in a small house situated near the crest of a hill from which when I walk up and over the crest, I can see a magnificent view of the Sea of Galilee. This is the very same area where Jesus walked and taught His disciples and the multitudes that followed Him here.

It would be difficult to end this chapter on why I believe in Jesus and how He ransomed me without hoping and praying that all who read this book will come to know God in their own very personal way through Jesus. I pray that those of you who do not know our Lord and Savior Jesus Christ will come into that wonderful and personal relationship with Him right now. And for those who do know and love Jesus, I pray you will now know Him more fully, experience Him more deeply, and see His glory in you and your families' lives from this moment on.

If you would like to receive Jesus into your life and come into the relationship with God He wants to have with you, please just ask Him now to come into your life. If you would like help with the words, then please pray this little prayer on the next page with me right now. Please do not wait a second longer.

Ransomed: Let the redeemed of the LORD say so...

"Dear Holy Father, I know I am a sinner and cannot save myself. Please forgive me of my sins. I believe Jesus is my Lord and Savior and that He died for me, paying the penalty for my sins, and that You raised Him from the dead that I may live with You forever. I want Jesus as the Lord of my life so that as Your Holy Spirit lives through me, I will please You as Jesus did. Thank You, Dear Father. I love and praise You. In Jesus' Mighty and Wonderful Name, Amen. I am now Your son/daughter!

Welcome to the Kingdom of God!

"Therefore, if anyone is in Christ,
he is a new creation; old things have passed away;
behold, all things have become new."
2 Corinthians 5:17

Halleluyah!!!

APPENDIX A

DEPRESSION: WHAT IS IT?

Depression is an illness. It is a "whole-body" illness, as defined by the National Institute of Mental Health, involving body, mind and spirit. It affects eating and sleeping, feelings about oneself, and thoughts about things. It affects mood and thoughts. It also attacks the spirit because of the helplessness and hopelessness it sometimes brings. A depressive disorder is not a passing "blue mood." It is not a sign of "personal weakness" or a condition that can be willed or wished away. Anyone with a depressive illness cannot merely "pull themselves together" and get better. Asking one to "snap out" of a depression makes as much sense as asking someone to "snap out" of diabetes or cancer. Without treatment, symptoms can last for weeks to years and eventually can lead to suicide. Appropriate treatment, however, can help over 80% of those who suffer from depression.

Basically, there are three major kinds of depression:

1) **Bipolar Depression** (manic-depressive illness) – A Manic-Depressive illness involves cycles of depression and elation or mania. Sometimes the mood switches are dramatic and rapid, but most often they are gradual. When in the depressed cycle, you can have any or all of the symptoms of a depressive disorder (see symptom list that follows). Mania often affects thinking, judgment, and social behavior in ways that cause serious problems and embarrassment. For example, unwise business or financial decisions may be made when in a manic phase.

2) **Dysthymia Depression** - A less severe type of depression, dysthymia involves long-term, chronic symptoms that do not disable, but keep one from functioning at "full steam" or from feeling good. Sometimes people with dysthymia also experience major depressive episodes.

3) **Major Depression** – Major Depression is manifested by a combination of symptoms (see symptom list that follows) that interfere with the ability to work, sleep, eat; and enjoy once-pleasurable activities. These disabling episodes of depression can occur once, twice, or several times in a lifetime.

Below are three main conditions, I believe, that can contribute to the cause of depression.

1. Poor personal choices can contribute to causing depression over a sustained period of time. Total dependency on drugs and alcohol is a major cause of depression, for example. Excessive drinking was certainly a contributing factor in causing depression in my case.
2. Severe Emotional Trauma (i.e., Death in the family, Abuse, Criticism/Rejection, Violence) are contributing factors.
3. A chemical depletion of Seratonin in the brain is linked to depression.

Interestingly enough the Bible is very clear about a main cause of depression and gives us what will help. God says in the Bible, *"Anxiety in the heart of man causes depression, But a good word makes it glad"* (Proverbs 12:25). I know from my own experience with depression how encouragement from family and friends always lifted me up, and still does.

In my circumstance leading up to my Major Depression, I ignored all these conditions and symptoms, thinking "I can handle this," but it almost killed me. That is because depression, such as I had, makes you have negative thoughts about yourself, about the world, the people in your life, and about the future. It is as if you are seeing yourself, the world, and the future through a fog of negativity. In reality, negative thoughts are not a rational or normal way to think of things. A person not suffering from depression would not accept negative thinking as being true. As my illness responded to treatment, this negative thinking disappeared.

Coupled with negative perceptions is the feeling that nothing can make the depression better. This is also a symptom of the illness itself. What I found out after treatment is that things were not hopeless as I thought they were. But because I did not seek treatment soon enough, I found that my negative (hopeless) view of the future led me to attempt suicide. If you have suicidal thoughts it is imperative to tell your pastor, rabbi, doctor, family member or friend about this and ask for help immediately. And take all suicidal comments from others very seriously, even if they are made in jest and get them help.

Other symptoms listed below can also signal depression. **If any of these symptoms are experienced over a continuous two-week period, it is necessary to seek professional treatment immediately:**

1. Persistent sad, anxious, or "empty" mood.
2. Feelings of hopelessness, pessimism.
3. Feelings of guilt, worthlessness, helplessness.

4. Loss of interest or pleasure in hobbies and activities that you once enjoyed,
including sex (in my marriage this was very true).
5. Insomnia, early-morning awakening, or oversleeping.
6. Lack of appetite and/or weight loss or overeating and weight gain.
7. Decreased energy, fatigue, being "slowed down."
8. Thoughts of death or suicide, suicide attempts (again, in my case very true).
9. Restlessness, irritability.
10. Difficulty concentrating, remembering, making decisions (or even praying, I found) .
11. Persistent physical symptoms that do not respond to treatment such as; headaches, digestive disorders, and chronic pain.

These are the danger signals for major depression. Unfortunately they are not always visible, even to the trained observer. That is why I try to discuss my experience every chance I get. As mentioned earlier, after one such discussion with a local youth group, two adolescents who attended my talk reported to their parents that they had similar symptoms. One was treated by their family physician the other was immediately taken to a hospital for treatment. This is just one example why it is extremely important to get as much information as possible about this illness and to talk about it with family and friends. If one cannot talk about it, that in itself is a danger signal.

We have to bring this illness out in the open. We cannot continue to deny that depression exists or it is only a sickness of the "weak" or the "indigent." This illness is so widespread that it is estimated to have touched every family in this country today. In fact, suicide is the number 7 killer in America. Suicide is also the number 2 killer (number 1 being accidents) among our young people (15-26) today. One in seven of our teenagers now seriously consider suicide.

If you think you might need help, seek your internist or general practitioner and explain your situation. Sometimes an actual physical illness can cause depression-like symptoms (a thyroid condition, for instance), so it is best to see your regular physician first to have a complete check up. Your doctor should be able to refer you to a psychiatrist, if the severity of your depression warrants it. Other sources of help include the members of the clergy (extremely important). Free depression screening is usually available in many communities by calling your Suicide Prevention Hot Line or check with your local hospital.

Finally, as for healing one's spirit, I have found that my reconciliation to God through Jesus Christ our Lord and Savior was the single most important step in my recovery process. From His help and that of my family, friends and the many fine professionals who treated me, I am here today to bring attention to this deadly malady and testify to the saving grace of God through Jesus Christ. Please do not make the mistake that I did by ignoring the signs. Reach out and receive the help that is there now, before it is too late.

APPENDIX B

HEALTH TIPS FOR SOUL AND BODY

First and foremost in staying fit spiritually and physically is having a right relationship with our Father in Heaven through Jesus Christ our Lord and Savior. Second, I believe, is having our priorities straight. The main priorities are (1) God; (2) family, friends, and others; and (3) ourselves in that order. Jesus gave us these priorities when He gave us the Two Greatest Commandments. He said, "'*You shall love* [1] ***the LORD your God*** *with all your heart, with all your soul, and with all your mind.' This is the first and great commandment. And the second is like it: 'You shall love* [2] ***your neighbor*** *as* [3] ***yourself***'" (Matt 22:37–40, emphasis mine).

That means we need to spend quality time with God, our family, friends, others and ourselves. I must confess, however, while writing this book this quality time has suffered. We should also remember those that are less fortunate than us and to support our place of worship. Jesus said, "*It is more blessed to give than to receive*" (Acts 20:35).

Next, our diet is extremely important. Spiritually I start and end every day in prayer and God's word, the Bible. The Bible is the bread of life. "*So He humbled you, allowed you to hunger, and fed you with manna which you did not know nor did your fathers know, that He might make you know that man shall not live by bread alone; but man lives by every word that proceeds from the mouth of the LORD*" (Deuteronomy 8:3).

Prayer is so important because it is choosing to have God in our life. Prayer does not mean we can ask for fancy clothes or extravagant material things and expect to get them. It also does not mean asking God for something with our answer for Him. First, prayer is our fellowship with God and confiding in Him. Secondly, prayer is petitioning God for the needs of others and us. When approaching God the Bible says, "*Enter into His gates with thanksgiving, And into His courts with praise. Be thankful to Him, and bless His name*" (Psalms 100:4). "*Now this is the confidence that we have in Him, that if we ask anything according to His will, He hears us. And if we know that He hears us, whatever we ask, we know that we have the petitions that we have asked of Him*" (1 John 5:14-15).

As far as natural foods go, I have found that certain foods are good for me and some that are not. Some of these foods that I noticed was while I was recovering because of the liquid diet that totally cleansed my system from the additives and preservatives that are in our processed food today. For example, as mentioned before there is even a warning label on most toothpaste today because of a toxin that can poison children under six.

Because my metabolism can be different from yours the foods I list may or may not affect you the same as me. In any case, consult your doctor or nutritionist to be sure. The main foods that affect me negatively are:

1) All carbonated drinks.
2) All caffeine drinks.
3) Any food with "whey" in it.
4) Sugar
5) Alcoholic drinks

Also it has been reported that the substance "aspartame," found in many diet drinks, has a negative effect on our nervous system. Consult your doctor before taking anything (food or drink) with this substance in it. Also, any non-doctor approved drugs are poison to our body, soul and spirit.

Now here are some foods that I have found have a positive effect on my system:

1) Turkey (a natural replacement for Seratonin)
2) Fish
3) Chocolate (A doctor's report I read on this said fish and chocolate helped in depression but they did not know why)
4) Honey (A natural antibiotic. **Children 3 and under should not take honey. Please consult your doctor first about your child taking honey.**)
5) Apples

The Bible also lists foods that are not good for us (Leviticus 11:1-23). I have found that since I have eliminated pork and shell fish, for example, my cholesterol level has gone from 275 at its highest point to around 175 now. In fact, when I had my last physical the doctor said my blood test was perfect.

Finally, be an encourager and pray for others continually. I don't know how many times an encouraging word from a family member or friend picked me up when I needed it most. And when someone said they were praying for me, that really gave me encouragement. The Bible tells us just how powerful encouraging words are. God says, ***"Pleasant words are like a honeycomb, Sweetness to the soul and health to the bones"*** (Proverbs 16:24).

"I will lift up my eyes to the hills--
From whence comes my help?
My help comes from the LORD,
Who made heaven and earth."
Psalm 121:1-2

The author may be reached at these addresses:

William Stewart Whittemore
PMB 8450, PO Box 2428
Pensacola, Florida 32513

Email: stewart33@earthlink.net

Be Blessed!